My Life Growing up White during Apartheid in South Africa

By Philip Hummel

authorHOUSE®

AuthorHouse™
1663 Liberty Drive
Bloomington, IN 47403
www.authorhouse.com
Phone: 1-800-839-8640

First published by AuthorHouse 1/21/2011

ISBN: 978-1-4567-1800-8 (sc)
ISBN: 978-1-4567-1801-5 (e)

Library of Congress Control Number: 2011900621

Printed in the United States of America

Table of Contents

Acknowledgments

I would like to thank all the ex-South Africans, family, and friends for all their personal information and facts, that made it possible for me to write this book.

Cover

Me with my nanny Anna on vacation in Cape Town 1956

Introduction

South Africa is a country of unimaginable beauty, especially Cape Town where I grew up. The beautiful Atlantic and Indian Oceans are complimented by beautiful fine white sand. The exquisite mountains nestle the city in magical storybook imagination, that can be equaled by no other country.

This book is a short collection of memories about living in South Africa during apartheid. I wrote this book for the reader to easily understand what it was like to live in this environment.

It is not a history lesson but some personal experiences that I went through living in South Africa at the time. Living through apartheid, I never even realized that it existed, because we were brought up to believe that it was normal. Growing up we were sheltered without knowing anything else .

Life was paradise for me and hell for others. Many of us did not know or care, and even if we did try to change the system, it would have resulted in prison or death.

Most white people chose not to get involved or rock the boat. We believed that changing apartheid would have caused the country to fall into the hands of the communists, and many white people were fearful that black rule would have destroyed South Africa and their lives.

The other side of the coin is that I can't even begin to understand what it was like for most blacks, which was excruciatingly difficult, something that I didn't know anything about, and did not experience.

I hope my story will make you understand why white people were extremely reluctant to change. Our history books never taught us anything good about blacks. I can't remember ever learning anything positive that blacks did. What I did learn was that they were lazy, uneducated, dangerous, and drank a lot. "Stay away from them, and if they bother you call the police!" Life for most of the whites was paradise. There are things that I have forgotten, and some names were changed. I know there were serious injustices in South Africa, but I loved growing up there.

Non-being

non-white
non-entity
I think but am not
but to think I am not
is to be
not what I can
but what I must
invisible
unseen
In shades of yellow, brown, and black
that fade in the white glare
of the being one

Muthal Naidoo

What was Apartheid?

Apartheid was a system of legal racial separation which dominated the Republic of South Africa from 1948 until 1993. Apartheid is an Afrikaans word meaning "separateness." The mechanisms of apartheid were set in place long before 1948, and South Africa continues to deal with the repercussions. Under apartheid, various races were separated into different regions, and discrimination against people of color was not only acceptable, but legally entrenched, with whites having priority housing, jobs, education, and political power. Although South Africa was heavily criticized for the system, it was not until 1991 that the legal system of apartheid began to break down, and in 1993 was thrown out altogether with the election of Nelson Mandela as the first democratically elected president of South Africa in 1994.

The country was colonized by the English and Dutch in the 17th century. There was English domination over the Dutch descendents (known as Boers or Afrikaners). The discovery of diamonds in these lands around 1900 resulted in an English invasion. Following independence from England, an uneasy power-sharing between the two groups held sway until the 1940's, when the Afrikaner

National Party was able to gain a strong majority. Strategists in the National Party invented apartheid as a means to cement their control over the economic and social system. Initially, the aim of apartheid was to maintain white domination while extending racial separation.

With the enactment of apartheid laws in 1948, racial discrimination was institutionalized. Race laws touched every aspect of social life, including a prohibition of marriage between non-whites and whites, and the sanctioning of black jobs. In 1950, the Population Registration Act required that all South Africans be racially classified into one of three categories: white, black (African), or coloured (of mixed decent). The coloured category included major subgroups of Indians and Asians.

Classification into these categories was based on appearance , social acceptance, and descent. A white person was defined as in appearance obviously a white person, or generally accepted as a white person. A person could not be considered white if one of his or her parents were black. A black person would be accepted as a member of an African tribe or race, and a coloured person is one that is not black or white. All blacks were required to carry 'pass books' containing fingerprints, a photo, and information on access to white areas.

Starting in the 60's, a plan of 'Grand Apartheid' was set up, emphasizing territorial separation and police repression.

The penalties imposed on political protest, even non-violent protest, were severe. During the states of emergency, which continued intermittently until 1989, anyone could be detained without a hearing by a low-level police official for up to six months. Thousands of individuals died in custody, frequently after gruesome acts of torture. Those who were tried were sentenced to death, banished, or imprisoned for life, like Nelson Mandela.

This is what we saw every day

Who are the Blacks

The Bantu group is the biggest, about 50 million people in Africa speak Bantu. There are about 200 different languages spoken, mostly Swahili and Zulu. Most of the Bantu speaking people came wandering from the north, and settled down in South Africa during the last 500 years. The original black population in South Africa were the bushmen, who belong to the Khoisan people. They speak a very special language with a lot of clicks.

Some of them are made with the tongue and can sound like a wet kiss. There are two groups of black languages in South Africa, Bantu languages and then the ones spoken by Khoisan people.

Who are the Coloureds and Indians?

The term 'Cape Coloureds' refers to the modern-day descendants of slave laborers imported into South Africa by Dutch settlers, as well as to other groups of mixed ancestry originating in the present-day of the Western Cape. They are the predominant population group found in the Western Cape Province. Their population size is roughly 4 million. Most Cape Coloureds' mother tongue is Afrikaans, as a result of their cultural development in the Dutch and Afrikaans-speaking areas of South Africa, but a minority are English speaking. Slaves of Malay ancestry were brought from Indonesia, Malaysia, and Madagascar. From these diverse origins they gradually developed into a group the coloured people (African and European origin) that was subsequently classified as a single major ethnical group under the Apartheid regime. In many cases the slaves were imported to be concubines and wives for single male Dutch settlers. People from India and the islands within the Indian

Ocean region were also taken to the Cape and sold into slavery by the Dutch settlers. The Indian slaves were almost invariably given Christian names but their places of origin were indicated in the records of sales and other documents, so that it was possible to get an idea of the ratio of slaves from different regions. These slaves were dispersed, and lost their cultural Indian identity in the course of time, hence being labeled Cape Coloureds. Much racial mixture has occurred over the generations, between the Europeans, Indians, Malays, and various Black tribes.

Technically, the term Cape Coloured referred to a subset of Coloured South Africans, with subjective criteria having been used by the Apartheid bureaucracy to determine whether a person was a Cape Coloured, or belonged to one of a number of other related "Coloured" subgroups such as the Cape Malays or "Other Coloureds". The term "Coloured" was used to distinguish people of mixed ancestry, paler South Africans of European descent, and the darker black South Africans. There were often exceptions to this generalization, and consequently Apartheid classifications often led to tragic-comic consequences, with some paler family members being classified as white and others coloured. This contentious classification had in the past no consistent meaning among South Africans – opinion, more than anything else, dictated who was classified as Cape Coloured. You can clearly understand the paranoia of the government and the insanity it created.

Who are the Whites?

South Africa's white population descendants were largely from the colonial immigrants of the late 17th, 18th, and 19th centuries. They were of Dutch, German, French Huguenot and British origins. Linguistically, divided into Afrikaans and English speaking groups, and also many small communities that had immigrated over the last century.

Religions

In terms of religious affiliation, about two-thirds of South Africans are Christian, mainly Protestant. They belong to a variety of churches, including many that combine Christian and traditional African beliefs. Many non-Christians espouse these traditional beliefs. Other significant religions are Islam, Hinduism, and Judaism.

Born in Upington

Map of South Africa- Upington and Cape Town

I was born on June 8, 1955 in Upington, South Africa a small town on the Orange River. My dad and his three brothers ran a large department store called 'Hummel Brothers'. None of their wives worked as many women didn't those days, especially White Jewish Women. They were supported by their husbands which was the custom during those times. Many women attended social functions, and did no housework.

**My dad second from the left and his 3 brothers
(family member in the middle) in front of
their store in Upington, early 1960's**

In Upington I had a black nanny Anna, who would look after me. She would feed me, take me for walks, and basically brought me up as her own child. Anna had a room that was behind our house and I don't remember ever seeing a bath or shower in her room. I was even carried on her back the way Africans carried their children. We loved our nannies!

We not only had Anna but also another domestic servant, her name was Troy who helped with cleaning, cooking, and other domestic chores. All white male adults were addressed as 'Baas' or boss by all blacks. I was referred to as 'Klein Baas' or small boss by all blacks, as were all other small white male children.

My first day of school 1961

Educational Field trip

I started kindergarten in Upington. My kindergarten teacher thought we should go on a field trip and see chickens getting slaughtered, teaching us to understand where the meat came from. I still remember the blades, blood, smell, and feathers everywhere.

I thank her for turning me into a vegetarian which I still am today, and the health benefits that go along with it!

Upington was in the country and very much like the deep south of the United States. Black people lived in the township outside the town and never came into the town unless they were working for whites, or had a very good reason.

The Police were not people you ever messed with, and you never said or did anything against the government in public. They had the power to kill you especially if you were black. Police wore light blue uniforms with a brown leather gun belt worn diagonally across their shoulder, and a cap that often reminded me of the SS of Nazi Germany. Life in Upington at the time was paradise for my family. I had uncles, aunts, and many cousins. We had a "braaifleis" (barbeques) almost every weekend and had many family gatherings. My dad was a big shot in the town because of his store, and he received a great deal of respect. Many people visited our house. Life for us was paradise but life for blacks was very difficult. There were some whites who would let their domestic servants sleep on the kitchen floor, having no regard for them as human beings. I also saw an article where a farmer would pay his black laborers with glasses of wine, and eventually got them addicted so that all they would care about was the wine.

**My family; Scampy, Me, Dad, Brenda, Mom
Upington, 1962**

As a child I would see black prisoners doing yard work around the town. They were guarded by a white policeman with a rifle and a whip, and a black policeman with a spear.

Black police were not allowed to carry guns and were loathed by other blacks as traitors. The police would arrest blacks for any reason and imprison them for as long as they needed them. A system of free labor was created! Yes, life was pretty great if you were white. Even though our servants worked in our houses and knew everything about our lives and families. We knew nothing about their personal lives or families. Most whites didn't care about their happiness or sadness. We expected them to be happy if we were happy and sad if we were sad . My family treated our servants with extreme human dignity. Some whites, did not consider black people human, and treated them very badly. If the police caught any blacks walking around the town for no reason they were picked up, often beat up badly, and imprisoned. Blacks were very careful to be extremely polite to whites, especially to the police.

The Beautiful City of Cape Town

Mountains of Cape Town

Moving to Cape Town

Around 1962 my dad decided he wanted to leave Upington and move to Cape Town, a beautiful city 500 miles south on the Atlantic Ocean. A large company called " The OK

Bazaars" wanted the Hummel Brothers building for their new store, or they were going to build their own. Hummel brothers knew it was time to get out so they sold their building, and our family was off to beautiful Cape Town with all our things and our loveable fox terrier, Scampy.

We drove down and sent all the rest of our stuff by train.

In Cape Town, English was the spoken language where as in Upington it was Afrikaans (similar to Dutch). Cape Town was less conservative. I use these words carefully, because this does not mean blacks were more welcome. My dad loved walking near the ocean so we eventually settled into a three bedroom apartment called Westridge in Mouille Point, an exquisite area on the coast, 100 yards from the ocean. There was an old lighthouse in Mouille Point. I used to like climbing to the top and look at the ocean. The lighthouse keeper would let me and a few friends go up to the top, about six floors. Mouille Point was directly across from Robben Island. As a young child I loved going down to the beach with my dog Scampy. There were plenty of rocks filled with fish, octopus, crabs, and many other sea creatures.

Me at age 11 with Scampy at Milton Pool, Sea Point

Scampy the Rat Catcher

Scampy was a fox terrier and they were bred for hunting rats. He loved going with me for walks on the beach.

Scampy hated going into water. One day while on the beach a big rat ran out from pieces of wood on the beach. Scampy immediately took off after the rat. The rat sensing the dog was after him ran across the rocks and dove into the water. Scampy hated water but he hated rats more, so in he dove after the rat. He eventually caught and killed the rat. He scrambled back onto the rocks with my help, not quite sure why he had just dived into the icy cold water. He was a great hunter for a small dog.

He was with us for fifteen years, and he died when I was seventeen years old . I loved that dog, and still remember how he enriched my life

Whites only on the beaches

The only blacks that were allowed on the beaches were domestic servants looking after white children, city workers, or ice cream venders. If any black person dared to venture onto a "Whites Only Beach" they were taking their lives into their hands, and would have been arrested. Blacks had their own beaches but they were far away from white areas. I loved the beaches in Cape Town, they were so beautiful! The blue cold Atlantic Ocean was like being in a dream, and you could see large ships passing by the beach, sailing around the southern part of Africa. I loved this area as a child.

**Me on a "Whites Only" beach in Sea
Point, Cape Town around 1964.**

Seeing Robben Island Everyday

Everyday I could see Robben Island about 7 miles across the ocean from Mouille Point. I always thought how amazing it would be to go over there on a raft or a canoe. I actually built one but it sank about 500 yards from the shore, and I had to swim back.

The water was extremely cold and there were very strong currents between the island and the mainland. As I got older I learned that Nelson Mandela the dangerous agitator was imprisoned on the island. I was happy that he was there because I was told that he was a very dangerous man and would endanger all the whites if he was set free or escaped.

Strange as it may be, my Uncle David was the doctor that took care of Mandela on Robben Island. I was young but I never heard any discussions in the house about Mandela, because it was forbidden and dangerous to do so. My Uncle David really admired Mandela, and was very depressed seeing him jailed on the island. I will write more about my Uncle David later.

In Cape Town I attended Sea Point Junior School which was only for boys. Only for white boys as no blacks were allowed to attend any white schools. Blacks had their own dilapidated schools which received a minuscule amount of money compared to the white schools. It was not in the interest of the government to educate blacks. They reckoned the poorer and less educated blacks were, the easier it would be to control them. Many black children did not have enough clothes, shoes, or food.

Black Body Builder Photo in my School Bag

One day I saw a photograph of a black body builder in the newspaper. I decided to cut it out and paste it on the inside of my clumsy big school suitcase, that I carried to school. I was going to show the other kids something cool! When I opened my suitcase to show the other kids they started laughing at me, telling me he was black and that I was stupid. As you can imagine when no one was looking I tore the photo off my bag, and never showed it to anyone again.

After completing elementary school a friend and I decided that we were going to burn all our books on the seawall across the road from where we lived. We poured gasoline on all our books and set them on fire. After they burned out we threw the ashes over the seawall into the ocean and cheered. At the time I thought that was coolest thing I had ever done. Wow, those were good times! There was no middle school, so it was off to high school at the age of thirteen.

Me second from left 16 with friends at my 11ᵗʰ grade High School Dance

Camps Bay High School

I went on to Camps Bay High School a beautiful school built in the mountains of Camps Bay. Looking out of the window you could see the Atlantic Ocean below.

Cape Town is one of the most beautiful places on Earth, with the city nestled in under the majestic Table Mountain. In fact every year a whale would come into one of the bays below our school and give birth. We could see this by just looking out of the classroom window which most of us took for granted. Yes, you guessed it boys and girls but only whites. We never socialized with blacks at any time in our lives as it was forbidden, and it was also considered subversive. Basically you knew your place in society and it was a great life, so why cause trouble. Even though we did not like the government we were secretly relieved that they were keeping the blacks out of our schools and neighborhoods.

Yes, deep down we did not want change out of fear what could happen.

The School Inspector

Another story my mom told me that stuck in my brain, was that a white school inspector, a retired principal was at a school somewhere in the country. He decided to read a poem that was written by a young black boy to all the students in a school assembly.

A brilliant poem that was well received by the school until he carelessly mentioned that it was written by a young black boy. The following day parents showed up at the school and demanded that the inspector be fired for reading a poem written by a black boy. The school inspector did something that was unforgivable in the eyes of the whites, making the black student appear smarter than the white children. I do not know what the outcome was, but I always wondered if he would have done that again knowing what happened. I think he would have!

Mandela on Robben Island

Mandela was arrested in 1962 and sentenced to 5 years imprisonment with hard labor. In 1963, when many fellow leaders of the African Nationalist Congress were arrested, Mandela was brought to stand trial with them for plotting to overthrow the government by violence. His statement from the dock received considerable international publicity. On June 12, 1964 Mandela and 8 of the accused were sentenced to life imprisonment.

During his years in prison, Nelson Mandela's reputation steadily grew. He was widely accepted as the most significant black leader in South Africa, and became a potent symbol of resistance as the anti-apartheid movement gathered strength. He consistently refused to compromise his political position to obtain his freedom. From 1964 to 1982 he was incarcerated on Robben Island Prison, about 7 miles from Cape Town. Mandela spent the next 18 years on Robben Island. In 1982 he was then transferred to Pollsmoor prison in Cape Town, and later to Victor Verster Prison, where it was discovered that he was suffering from tuberculosis.

Mandela was released from jail on Sunday February 11, 1990. The first images of the president-to-be walking out of prison were relayed live via satellite to ecstatic audiences across the world. Nelson Mandela was sworn in as the first black president of South Africa in 1994, thus ending the Apartheid era.

Mandela spent 18 years in prison on Robben Island

My Uncle David

My mother grew up in a small town in South Africa called Neuvatville in the Cape Province. She had two sisters and four brothers. Her oldest brother Aaron had to take the role of her father, because he died when she was eleven.

Moving on to WWII my Mom became a nurse with the rank of lieutenant. Her brother David became a doctor. Both my mother and her brother David were to remain in South Africa during the war to help injured soldiers who were sent back to recuperate in South Africa. My Mom also nursed many Italian soldiers who remained in South Africa after the war.

After WWII my Uncle who was very sympathetic toward the black cause in South Africa opened a practice in District Six, a famous suburb of Cape Town mainly coloured. Even though Uncle David was white the people there loved him because they knew how much he cared about them.

After the war my uncle hurt his back and started using morphine, and eventually became addicted.

My Mom's other brother, my Uncle George, who managed a hotel, was a go getter, knew General Van Denberg' a top official in the South African Police. He warned my Uncle George that they were going to arrest my Uncle David. George got David into rehab. in a place called Gramestown as quickly as he could, and also secured him a job as the District Surgeon for the police in Cape Town. The police were very conservative and the enforcers of apartheid. As ironic as life is, my Uncle David got the job examining Nelson Mandela and other political prisoners on Robben Island. He had landed a job that would get him intimately close to all these people he admired so much.

Robben Island Nelson Mandela's prison for 18 years 7 miles from Cape Town.

My Uncle was a very sensitive and wonderful human being who was very depressed about seeing Mandela and the others on the island, wasting their lives away. He would never speak about it openly to the family, because it was extremely dangerous to do so. Sadly my Uncle David couldn't break his addiction and committed suicide by jumping to his death from his apartment building. The family is not sure why he did this, but some assumed that some of these factors influenced him

My Uncle David, Nelson Mandela's Doctor on Robben Island

The 'Homelands' (A way to make blacks non citizens in their own country)

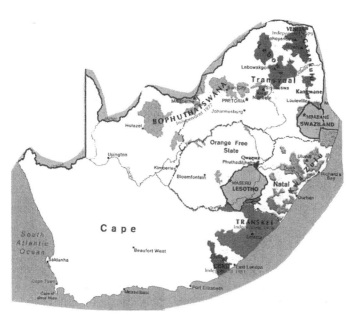

Shaded areas were the homelands in SouthAfrica

In 1951, the Bantu Authorities Act established a basis for ethnic government in African reserves, known as the 'homelands.' These homelands were independent states to which each black person was assigned by the government according to the record of origin (which was frequently inaccurate). All political rights, including voting, held by a black were restricted to the designated homeland. The idea was that they would be citizens of the homeland, losing their citizenship in South Africa and any right of involvement with the South African Parliament, which held complete control over the homelands. From 1976 to

1981, four of these homelands were created, denationalizing nine million blacks. Nevertheless, Africans (blacks) living in the homelands needed passports to enter South Africa, becoming aliens in their own country.

Husbands and wives were separated causing many domestic problems. What a great way to show that proportionally to whites there were less blacks in South Africa, it was an ingenious idea even though diabolic!

Education

Prime Minister Hendrik Verwoerd

The *Bantu Education Act of 1953* was instituted to provide black pupils with different expectations and future goals than white students. These differences were incorporated to make sure that blacks had different syllabi and schooling facilities than white children. For black students, the emphasis of their education was placed on technical education, equipping them for practical work as opposed to the education received by white students, equipping them for a professional job. The job reservation laws set aside the elite jobs and professions for whites.

According to Prime Minister H.F. Verwoerd, <u>*"the only way blacks would be tolerated near white areas was if there were some need that had to be carried out."*</u> Blacks were primarily trained to become artisans, tradesmen, and semi-skilled laborers. Their only reason for being, according to government theory, was to be of maximum benefit to the national economy. Only a few of the black students in the public schools aspired beyond their mediocre training to higher education levels. Those who did were segregated into black universities under the *Extension to University Education Act*. Only 14 percent of black students reached secondary schools, and even fewer furthered their education to the university level. It was also illegal for blacks to employ whites for any type of work.

On September 6, 1966, Verwoerd was assassinated in Cape Town, shortly after entering the House of Assembly at 2:15 p.m.. A uniformed parliamentary messenger named Dimitri Tsafendus stabbed Verwoerd in the neck and chest four times before being subdued. Verwoerd was rushed to Groote Schuur Hospital, but was declared dead upon arrival.

Serving a Black Man in a Restaurant

I was about seventeen and decided I wanted a summer job. Being a vegetarian, I decided to apply for a job at Irma's Vegetarian Restaurant. Irma was different, she was a tough no nonsense white women who made everything from scratch in her restaurant. I can still taste the amazing bread she made, and remember the food being so good that eating dinner there was payment enough. Irma told us that she had black friends, and that if any of them came into her restaurant we were to serve them.

Well as you can guess a young black man and his date came into the restaurant to eat. Yep, I was the waiter and excited. I worried how this was going to turn out. Walking up to the table I sensed that he was very uncomfortable, and suddenly everything was reversed. I, a young white male was serving a black man. You may say so what, but back then it was something extremely exciting, and terrifying at the same time. I approached his table and said, "Good evening sir, can I take your order." He looked at me in shock and nervously ordered. I can say that I was shaking and sweating realizing this was an amazing and exciting moment for me. I felt that this guy was just like me, and enjoyed what I enjoyed. I have never forgotten that moment and even after many years I still smile thinking about how exciting it was during those times.

For years afterwards I wondered how he must have felt growing up during Apartheid and me being his waiter.

Getting Banned and Black Beauty

More than 2,000 people were banned in South Africa from 1950 to1990, labeled a communist or terrorist, or otherwise a threat to security and public order. The banned person would in effect be a public nonentity, confined to his or her home, not allowed to meet with more than one person at a time (other than family), hold any offices in any organization, speaking publicly or writing for any publication. Also barred from certain areas, buildings, and institutions, such as law courts, schools, and newspaper offices. A banned person could not be quoted in any publication.

In 1965 the government banned the book Black Beauty because it used the words "black" and "beauty" in the title. Of course, there aren't any black people in the book, since it is set in 19th century in England. During Apartheid, they assumed the book was some kind of black rights novel. The censer did not even read it he just didn't like the title.

The book is actually about animal rights and Black Beauty is a horse. Although grimly menacing, the magnitude of censorship and banning of expressions in South Africa during the Apartheid Regime seems truly paranoid. The comprehensive list of banned items included any object carrying ANC (African National Congress) symbols, buttons, T-shirts, and lighters, as well as objectionable literature, posters, and films, etc. The power to ban publications was held by the minister of the interior under the Publications and Entertainments Act of 1963. Under the act a publication could be banned if it was found to be "undesirable" for any of many reasons, including obscenity, moral harmfulness, blasphemy, causing harm to relations among sections of the population, safety, general welfare, peace, or order of the state. Thousands of books, newspapers, and other publications were banned in South Africa from 1950 to 1990. In1966 South Africa banned the Beatles records because of the remark John Lennon made that the band was 'more popular than Jesus'!

They were allowed to be played on the radio, but you could not buy their records in any store. The radio DJs would say, "Here is 'Let it Be' by the band I am not allowed to mention."

Also the movie, 'The Rocky Horror Picture Show' was banned after been screened for about six months. I saw it three times and then it was banned, pretty funny!

The book Black beauty was banned

TV in South Africa

On July 20, 1969 millions of South African families were huddled around a crackling radio, listening to the moonwalk. Nobody in the entire country could watch it on TV. Television was considered a criminal technology under apartheid.

Yes, the joys of radio, I spent hours as a child listening to the radio. Even now I like listening to the radio before I go to bed, my wife thinks I am crazy but how can she understand, she grew up in the USA. I know her parents would have understood!

I saw the moonwalk in South Africa, yes I saw it with my family about two weeks later on a TV taped format set up at the University of Cape Town, in a lecture hall for the public. We all thought it was so amazing even me, a boy of about fourteen.

First official TV broadcast in 1976

The main reason South Africa did not have TV until 1976 was that the government was afraid it would destroy apartheid. They realized how powerful a medium TV was and how quickly it could influence a large group of people, especially with a moving picture, as the saying goes in this case a moving picture is worth more than a thousand words. Yes, they could use it to their benefit too, but when there were so many untruths coming from the government, they would have had a difficult time finding propaganda footage for TV. Many thoughts were that the communists would try to bring down the South African way of life. When television finally came to South Africa, it definitely opened the eyes of many South Africans, even though most of the first shows were nature shows. I remember coming home from the army on a pass and I would sit for hours watching nature shows, funny now but I was hypnotized then. Most, if not all South Africans got color TV's when they became legal to own.

The technology was there just not the televisions.

Marnie my Malay friend

The Malays are an ethnic group or community in Cape Town, South Africa. The Dutch brought them from India and Indonesia starting around 1654 as slaves, and were the first group that introduced Islam to South Africa.

Marnie was a thin dark skinned guy with jet black hair and very good looking. We met at an interracial party which I will write about later in the book. Marnie and I became good friends. There was only one problem and that was that we could not go to the movies, a restaurant, the beach or any other public place together. In fact if he came to my house and somebody reported us, the security police would show up at the door with questions about why he was at the house.

One night I went to my girlfriend Susan's house. We had to pass the living room to her bedroom. Her parents were entertaining their friends when we walked by. Five minutes later Susan's mother called her and told her that Marnie could not be in their house. I sincerely do not believe that her parents minded him being there, they were more afraid of the police finding out.

Marnie not only had problems from whites, blacks would insult him too with, "Moenie vit raak nie - stop trying to act white!"

Well, we were young and willing to take chances. We hid him in our cars and in big groups, so that it was difficult for people to see him. I would go into a restaurant and buy food for him, then take it back to the car. All the girls liked Marnie because he was charming and good looking, yes white girls too, but there was a danger--- *The Immorality Act*. No whites or blacks could date or even consider dating each other, or engage in any kind of sexual contact. If you were caught you could be charged under the Immorality Act and be sent to prison, so we had to be very careful. Going to the beach with Marnie was a drag. Clifton is one of the most beautiful beaches in the world with hundreds of steps from the road to the beach. Yes, you are correct Marnie was not allowed on the beach because it was a white beach. I would run down to see if any of my friends were there (no cell phones those days). If they were, I could not stay because Marnie was on top by himself. This happened on many occasions and because of these difficulties it was extremely difficult to be friends. Sadly I must admit because of these incidences our friendship waned and I lost contact with him.

Marriage, Relationships and the Immorality Act

The laws dealing with personal rights during apartheid were so extensive and invasive that even inside the black townships, married couples and their families were required by law to obtain state permission before they could live together. Authorities had every right to deny such permission if the families of black workers were considered to be "surplus blacks." Families labeled "surplus" were forced to leave the Bantustans, (a territory set aside for black inhabitants) thus decreasing the number of blacks living near the white-zoned areas. Under the Immorality Act of 1950 and the Mixed Marriages Act of 1949, marrying a person of a different race was illegal. In addition, with the enactment of the Immorality Amendment Act of 1957, showing or even having intentions to have any type of relationship between members of a different race became a crime, punishable by imprisonment.

Transportation

In Cape Town public transport was very good. Buses were segregated, whites downstairs blacks upstairs, or even separate buses. If an older black person got on the bus, and could not climb the stairs they had to get off or sit at the back of the bus to the disgust of some passengers. I never heard black people protest they just accepted it.

Most of the buses that were used for blacks were not used for white passengers, because they were considered dirty!

Protesting could get you into a lot of trouble. If you were for black rights you were considered a communist, or someone trying to bring down the government. This was not looked upon kindly by the courts, and you could suddenly find yourself being watched, losing your job or in extreme personal danger. On the other hand if you did not do anything considered subversive, life for whites was amazing. Now there were people who were against apartheid, some openly protesting and others secretly working to end apartheid. Any way you look at this it was extremely dangerous and most people were afraid to get involved.

Very few blacks owned cars because they did not have enough money to keep the cars in good working condition, so it was easy to spot a black person's vehicle.

Transportation by bus from town to town, or city to city was another form of transportation, like Greyhound in the USA. The buses were comfortable with roomy seats and a lot of leg space. Behind the bus was a hitched trailer that was towed by the bus. In it were wooden seats for all the black passengers. There was no communication between the driver and the trailer, so if a black person wanted to stop for a bathroom break or an emergency there was no communication with the driver. The truth is that many whites did not care about the blacks.

It was very dehumanizing, and the government knew exactly what they were doing!

Blacks had to be extra careful where they traveled to in certain parts of the country, because they could find themselves in prison or serious personal danger.

Bus for blacks only

Music from the United States and South Africa

In South Africa we did not have television until 1976 so radio was our way of getting a great deal of our information. We would listen to music from the United States but many times did not know that some of the musicians and singers were black. I am sure that is why they were allowed to be played. I only realized this after I left South Africa.

Percy Sledge the soul singer came to South Africa in 1970, and was extremely well received. My Mom took my sister and I to see him at the Three Arts Theatre in Cape Town, whites only audience . He also performed for black audiences, but I am amazed that he was allowed to enter South Africa during apartheid. Black dignitaries and famous artists were allowed to stay in 'white hotels' because of their status.

Percy Sledge was the 'King of Soul in South Africa' and became a major cult figure as well. His appeal was so widespread that the Pepsi Cola Company asked him to launch a new soda drink called 'TEEM'. This resulted in the release of a promotional record with Percy Sledge singing about the joys of drinking 'TEEM'. This disc contained two radio-commercials and the full version of the tune, produced for South Africa exclusively.

Percy Sledge in South Africa Poster 1970

Many blacks liked Elvis because he sounded like he was black, and also because it was difficult for them to get hold of other black artists from the US.

Many of the South African Black singers have the most amazing voices in the world. If ever you have an opportunity to listen to their harmonies you will understand. Sadly, no black singers had an opportunity to make records in those days. It was very difficult to become a famous singer even for whites at the time. The government would never have allowed this to happen because of internationalism, and the fear of world opinion about Apartheid.

Sports in South Africa and my Uncle Abe

Rugby was the white man sport, and soccer the black man's sport. Both these sports were played by both blacks and whites, but more blacks played soccer. Blacks did follow the rugby games especially when there were test games. (games against other countries). The venue for these rugby games in Cape Town, were at the Newland's rugby stadium. South Africa's national teams are called 'Springboks' after the agile deer that lives there. South Africa was a powerhouse rugby country, even though there were only about 3 million whites in the country and the National team was exclusively white.

I remember watching the Lions from England play South Africa in 1974. The black fans were separated from the whites. Every time England scored the blacks would cheer. They did this for two reasons; first was to make all the whites angry, and the second was their way of protesting against Apartheid. South Africa was banned from the Olympics in 1964 because of Apartheid, and reinstated in 1996. My Uncle Abe below was a Junior Springbok Rugby Player and an incredible athlete. They played very few test games in those days. If it was in today's sports world with many more games and competitions, he would definitely have played in test games. In the paper of the time they mentioned him as being the 'burly Jewish player', something that would not have been written in today's politically correct world.

**My Uncle Abe: A phenomenal athlete was a
Junior Springbok Rugby Player around 1950**

Abe Hummel's Try Upsets Rhodesian Currie Cup Hopes

**One of the many article headings
that were written about him**

Getting back to my story, around 1969 I was talking
to this coloured man who was fishing off the seawall in
Mouille Point where I lived. He had heard about my
Uncle Abe. He told me that if blacks were on the team,
the Springboks would have been much better. Me being
about thirteen or fourteen convinced that whites were
much better at everything, told him that I didn't think
that was true. It was many years ago, and I still think about

what I had said to him, and how he must have felt speaking to this kid who didn't know anything.

During Apartheid there were only whites in all international sports at the time. South Africa produced many world class athletes, out of a population of about 3 million. A truly amazing achievement!

The South African Police

The police were not to be 'messed with', and you tried to steer clear of them at any time, especially if you were political and/or black. Most of the police were Afrikaners and they took their job very seriously. You could say South Africa was a police state but by being white and staying out of politics you were pretty much left alone most of the time. South Africa wanted to know where black people were at all times, so blacks had to carry a pass that had to be produced on demand by the police. If a pass was out of order or lost the person was taken to the police station and dealt with! That could have meant been beaten up, thrown in prison, or even worse!

The police would drive around in vans that could transport prisoners. Many blacks were roughed up by the police before being thrown in the back of these vans.

I remember walking down the road in Sea Point one Saturday night around 1971 and saw a white driver knock down a black pedestrian. When the police arrived they found the white driver drunk and angry that his front fender was damaged. The police assessed the situation released the white driver and took the black pedestrian off to prison. I can remember seeing blacks looking on, and I remember seeing the anger in their eyes. Here is a sad joke that reflects the situation of the time, but quite relevant :

A white driver crashes into two black pedestrians, one is knocked fifty yards from the car the other one goes through the car's windshield and lands up in the back seat. The police come and charge the first one for fleeing the scene, and the second for breaking and entering.

It is a sad joke, but things like this happened continuously.

The South African Police would shoot first and then ask questions later, they were not afraid of being brought before a court or losing their jobs. If they killed someone, *then they killed someone*-end of story! Obviously not every police officer was a cold hearted killer but many were very brutal!

Whenever a political prisoner was captured I remember reading in the newspaper that he had committed suicide a few days later by jumping out of his cell window which was always on the 6th floor, or that he fell down the stairs hit his head and died, or while trying to escape was shot and killed.

These prisoners always seemed to jump out of the window on the 6th floor which mysteriously had no bars on the windows! Case closed!

This is the South Africa we knew, trusted and even loved! It was a perfect world for most of us whites!

Absolute fear of the police

In Mouille Point where I lived was a gas station about 50 yards from my house. I used to go there and get gas for my motorbike. Working at the gas station was this enormous black man. He was about six feet seven inches tall.

As big as this guy was he was petrified of the police.

**Blacks killed by the police during an
Anti-Apartheid protest in 1960**

He knew that the South African Police tortured people on a regular basis, and was deadly afraid of them! For some reason that day the police arrived at this gas station, jumped out of their vehicle grabbed, beat, and kicked him. They then threw him head first into the back of their police van. I saw him a week later both his eyes were bruised and he had a slight limp. The police had beaten him up for some reason of their own, instilling fear into anyone who disrespected them or the law. That is the way the South African Police operated.

Being Black in White South Africa

Blacks in South Africa during the height of apartheid definitely felt inferior. Everything good was white and everything bad was black. Blacks could see what whites had and compared it with what they had. They had nothing in their own country, and no matter how hard they worked they could never achieve what the whites had. Many blacks had a sense of hopelessness for their future. Whites in turn saw them as being lazy, and a catch 22 situation ensued. This could never be changed, the only way was to give blacks more rights, and this was never going to happen under Apartheid. Most white men viewed black women as unattractive because many of the them, (not coloured or Indian women) were overweight.

Black men considered it more attractive, and believed heavier women to be more healthy and able to bear healthier children. Every commercial was geared towards whites, such as food, clothing, and recreation. It was almost if blacks did not exist in this world. Not only did the whites not care, they believed blacks did not want these things or care about them. I am sure you are starting to understand the mentality of 'most' whites in South Africa at the time.

Racism was not a word that ever came up, it was just the way things were during apartheid.

I am sure if you asked many South Africans if they were racists during apartheid, they would have answered no, and would have proceeded to tell you how well they treat their servants. Telling you how they gave them a day off every two weeks and how they gave them leftovers from the family dinner. Never did they realize that blacks wanted exactly what they wanted, but whites did not know how to understand this. It was a way of life branded into the whites and blacks from a very young age. Cross the line and the punishment was severe.

Many blacks accepted their lot in life but many would say, "My children will not!" This was in the 1970's.

I remember hearing this, and it would send a chill down the backs of many whites. They could never imagine a South Africa being ruled by blacks, fearing a total destruction of the country. I must admit I remember that fear too!

Children begging for Food on the Railway Tracks

Another unimaginable sadness from the Apartheid era was that when I was very young, my Mom would take my sister and I on vacation by train from Upington to Cape Town, a two day journey. While stopping in desolate areas in the countryside many small young black children would come up to the train in tattered dirty clothes with no shoes, and beg for food. You could see how hungry and thin they were. This was one of the evils and travesties of the Apartheid Regime. As an adult thinking back I ask myself the question, how did the government allow this to go on. There is no answer, they just did.

Black and White Housing

In the photo below you can see the poverty in a black township of Cape Town during Apartheid. Table Mountain is in the background. There is nothing more to write, the photo tells it all! This is the poverty that blacks lived in while whites enjoyed a privileged lifestyle.

Black Poverty

This photo below is a house in Cape Town. It is below the mountain. Not every house had a pool or looked like this, but if you were white and had an average paying job you could afford a nice house.

A white neighborhood

The word 'Kaffir'

The original meaning is heathen, unbeliever or infidel, from the Arabic word Kaffir, and is still being used with this meaning by Muslims. The word kaffir is simply applied to anyone who is not a Muslim.

In South Africa during apartheid, the word had a primal derogatory tone, worse than the word nigger used towards blacks in the USA. I personally heard it being used by Afrikaners more than English speaking people, but I don't want to allege that as being completely correct.

At one time while wandering what I should do for a career and being a little confused about my future, I joined a company called Globe Engineering. I was going to work on the pistons of ships the size of a bedroom in a house. On one particular morning I arrived at work with my Globe Engineering jump suit, and plastic lunchbox ready for work. Next to me were some Afrikaners sitting around and waiting for work to start. Well at that moment three black workers came around the corner and walked by us. Suddenly I heard "More Kaffirs, good morning kaffirs." One of the black workers spun around with murder in his eyes while all the Afrikaners started laughing still continuing to drink their coffee.

The other two blacks restrained their friend from attacking the whites, because they realized what the consequences of his actions would be.

Also in the South African army I heard the word kaffir being used a great deal.

As a white growing up in South Africa I had no clue where the word came from but instantly knew that it was a deep painful insult used against blacks by some whites in South Africa.

In fact it was used by Afrikaners as a way of talking about their black farm workers. For example, "Waar is die Kaffirs vandag", where are the kaffirs today? They would use it in those terms not meaning to be mean, but as everyday language, and that it was okay to do so! I think some of the workers even accepted it as colloquial language.

The Afrikaans term '*Kaffir-boetie*' or (Kaffir Brother) was often used to describe a white person who fraternized with, or sympathized with the black community.

The Hated Pass Laws

A passbook that granted blacks into white areas

One of the most repressive apartheid restrictions was the law requiring blacks and all other nonwhites to carry a "pass book" stating their legal residence and workplace. Those without the proper papers could be stopped by police and immediately expelled to 'black areas'.

Interracial marriage and 'Immorality Acts' prohibited marriage and sexual relations across color lines.

The Group Areas Act defined residential areas by race.

Under it, Coloured and Indians were removed to special segregated townships. The Bantu Education Act gave the central government control of African (black) education, and closed private schools for blacks and forced them to attend a separate and inferior education system.

Hendrik Verwoerd the Prime Minister from 1958 until his assassination in 1966, stated that Native (black) education should be controlled in accordance with the policy of the state. "If the native (black) in South Africa today in any kind of school in existence is being taught to expect that he will live his adult life under a policy of equal rights, he is making a big mistake ." There is no place for him in the European community above the level of certain forms of labor. Can you even comprehend this being said or written about today?

The University Act segregated higher education sharply. It prohibited established universities to accept black students except by special cabinet permission.

The 1953 Reservation of Separate Amenities Act permitted the systematic segregation of train stations, buses, movie theaters, hotels, and virtually all other public facilities, and barred the courts from overturning such restrictions.

**Soldiers checking passbooks to stop blacks from
entering white areas without permission**

Crazy Rules of Apartheid

Apartheid, in its craziness, stated that blacks could not use white public toilets, but were allowed to clean those same toilets. Under apartheid, blacks could work in restaurant kitchens, prepare food, put it on plates and deliver it to the white patrons' tables, but could not eat that food at the same table in the restaurant. This is crazy if you think about it, also extremely hypocritical. If the government really believed in the separation of races then blacks should not even have worked in the restaurants at all.

Apartheid didn't go that far, it was built upon the premise that blacks did all the work, and for very little money. Now we can ask the question why were blacks allowed to do the work?

Why did the whites trust blacks that they had put into servitude, with their children, their food, and many other precious things in their lives. Some of the answers were that blacks needed the work even if the pay was extremely low. There was a fear by blacks that they would be punished severely for trying to injure whites. Many whites never dreamed that blacks would harm them, they understood that the black man and women appreciated them for the jobs they were given, 'also for civilizing them'.

Basically most whites were completely thoughtless about black aspirations. I am not accusing them of being insensitive even though they were. They were just doing what they were taught their whole lives.

Many may disagree and say nonsense, they should have been more sensitive. It is easy to judge this situation from the outside looking in, and from another country, and time in history. It is difficult to understand the mentality of that time. Most South Africans that look back now are ashamed of the past. As much justification as it takes to understand the evils of Apartheid it will never make people understand how crazy it was.

Mixed Racial Parties in Cape Town

When I was about 18 or 19 I started going to multiracial parties in the Cape Quarter of Cape Town, because I thought it was cool. These parties were strictly forbidden, but for some reason the police would turn a blind eye.

They were only in a certain areas, sort of bohemian, and mostly young people attended. I dared not tell my parents because I did not want to frighten them. There was a lot of marijuana at these parties, not that it was my thing but it was there. I am sure that the police had informers that were trying to get information by mingling in with the crowd. Maybe that is why the police turned a blind eye. It was very exciting because it was forbidden, and it made you feel like you were doing something that nobody in the country was doing, sort of special. There were some hookups between whites and blacks, and that was potentially dangerous. They would only hang out together in these areas, and would never dare to venture anywhere else together.

That would be like asking to be beaten up, and/or thrown into prison. They had to be extremely careful!

My Friend Neil Almost Got us Killed

Neil was the cool guy, he introduced me to Frank Zappa and Jimi. Since he had just gotten his driver's license, Neil wanted to drive all his buddies around town. He decided that he was going to buy some marijuana in this dangerous area. It was a weekend and we drove to this place that Neil claimed he had heard about. As we stopped this coloured guy walked up to the car and said, " Would you gentlemen like to score." Next minute a brick hit the back windshield and these guys start shouting, " Whitey get the fuck out of here!" Neil got nervous and stalled his stick shift car, as bricks started hitting the car from all directions. We got stuck again thinking that we were going to get stabbed to death. He got the car started and drove about 20 feet, stalled again, but eventually got us out.

We were all shaking and laughing about what had happened, relieved to have gotten out alive. We all knew what would have happened if he had stalled again. Those were fun days!

Jews, Religion, and Apartheid

Being Jewish myself and knowing our history about Russia, where most of the South African Jews immigrated from, and also the history of the holocaust. How did South African Jews accept apartheid?

I write this without any bias, South African Jews were extremely humane to their servants compared with most of the white population. Yes, I write servants but how did they accept Apartheid with their terrible history of abuse? I think many South African Jews had no first hand connection with Russia or the holocaust, and eased into this easy way of life. How did the Rabbi, Priest, or Minister justify his job being kind and loving to all people? Well I do understand human nature, and people have a subtle way of adapting and justifying what they do.

If not, how could they live with themselves. I know that in the Dutch Reformed Church (The church of many government officials) they would justify it from passages in the Bible such as these; that Apartheid denied blacks full participation based on doctrinal beliefs, that whites are pure, while black-skinned people are unrighteous, despised and loathsome descendants of the biblical Cain, who was cursed for killing Abel, and therefore were condemned to being cursed because of their blackness. Blacks were not allowed to attend any white churches, which were also separated. Many Afrikaners were repulsed by the presence, and any type of physical contact with blacks.

The Afrikaners were extremely religious and felt that what they were doing was something that God wanted, and if that is what God wanted, that was what they were going to do! Many of them were also anti-Semitic, but if they knew you personally or liked you as an individual they would say, "You are different."

My dad was considered a 'Boere Jood', translated a Jewish Afrikaner. This meant that he was born in the country grew up there, was white, and did not look Jewish. He could speak Afrikaans like a local, and could fit in easily.

At the end of the day he had to come home to his Jewish world, and probably saw many things that he had conflict with. He definitely came across a great deal of anti-Semitism but had to deal with it. My dad being the oldest son of eight children dropped out of school, and at the age of 13 had to work and help support his family.

There were many Jews who did oppose Apartheid, and risked their lives to change the system. I am not saying all the Jews accepted apartheid because they did not.

I personally did not realize or think about apartheid being good or bad. I never discussed it or thought about it. All I wanted to do was to go to parties and hang out with my friends. We looked but we never saw, we listened but we never heard, and worse of all we didn't care.

We were not mean or cold hearted we were trained to think like that.

Yes, trained not to get involved when life was paradise.

Many White South Africans must think about this today.

For me my eyes opened after I left the country, as if a spell was lifted.

South African Jews could have been described as being mostly mildly liberal and generally supported opposition parties. There were those that supported the United Party, then the Liberal Party, and some the ruling National Party.

The community as a whole was not aligned with any sort of violent revolutionary elements although there were some prominent South African Jewish socialists. The prime example of the more moderate approach was that of the highly-assimilated Harry Oppenheimer (1908–2000), born Jewish but converted to Anglicanism upon his marriage, the richest man in South Africa and the chairman of the De Beers Corporations. He was a supporter of the liberal Progressive Party and its policies, believing that granting more freedom and economic growth to South Africa's Black African majority was good politics, and a sound economic policy. The banner for this cause was held high by Helen Suzman, as the lone Progressive Party member in South Africa's parliament, representing the voting to many wealthy Jewish families at the time. She was also hated by many South Africans as a communist agitator. Many Jews did not care for her, and were also embarrassed by her being Jewish.

Despite the over-representation of Jews in the struggle against apartheid, the Jewish establishment and the majority of South African Jews remained focused on Jewish issues. Many individuals were unsupportive of the anti-apartheid cause, and communal institutions remained distant from the struggle against racial injustice until relatively late. A few rabbis spoke out against apartheid early, but they failed to gain support, and it was not until 1985 that the rabbinate as a whole condemned apartheid.

Again, where were they? They were afraid of their communities, and they were afraid of the government. If they said or did anything against apartheid they would have endangered themselves and their communities. I know that many Rabbis and Christian leaders supported and aided the black community secretly. They remembered the holocaust and pogroms of Russia but also feared black rule. They were in a pickle, at times being blamed for apartheid by whites and at other times by blacks. As the old saying goes: "The whites hate the blacks, the blacks hate the whites, and everybody hates the Jews." Jews in South Africa worked extremely hard to make life wonderful for their children, and many did. Many Jews enjoyed a very privileged life in South Africa. Below are both my grandparent's weddings as Jews of South Africa. Both sets of grandparents were born in Russia. They celebrated their weddings in the rural areas of South Africa. At the time many Jews lived in the countryside, but later moved to the cities. Many Jews may have been against Apartheid but they feared endangering their communities and families. It would also be fair to say that there were Jews who resisted the regime. Some paid for it with their lives!

My Dad's parents wedding 1912

My Mom's parents wedding 1909

The Army

I was training for war in Upington 1975

I barely finished high school because all I could do was think about girls and playing my guitar. After graduating I had no clue what I wanted to do so I went to the Cape Technical College to study electronics which was something I was interested in at the time. The campus was in the city, and I spent a year there and bombed. I failed most of my classes but did pass physics. I dropped out and before I knew it my draft papers were in the mail. A few weeks later I was on my way to the 8th South African Infantry Base in Upington with my girlfriend Susan crying hysterically at the railway station. I think she found a new boyfriend a week later.

Susan, my girlfriend two weeks before I was drafted

Yes, I was going back to my place of birth, Upington. If I forgot to mention it, Upington is the beginning of the hot Kalahari Desert with a distinctive red sand which I would run, crawl, and train in for the next few months.

When we arrived in Upington there were Bedford trucks at the station ready to take us to the army base. After we arrived at the base they lined us up and everybody got a haircut. We were issued with everything we needed as new recruits. In an instant life became depressing, there was sand everywhere, and we lived in tents with no heating. Temperatures were so low that water would freeze at nights until the sun came up, and then it boiled.

During the first week we hardly got enough food to eat and I lost 35 pounds in the first month. Later I found out that the career army people living in Upington were stealing most of the food and giving the spoiled remains to us, the new recruits. It was very hard to train with sub standard food. A few guys tried to commit suicide by cutting their wrists, and smashing their heads into the walls of the shower. When the army found out they were charged with damage to government property, and jailed. You were considered government property and if you injured yourself on purpose you were charged with damaging government property.

Our cold hearted drill sergeants would treat us like 'hell' using wonderful expletives and sayings to motivate us. I will write them in English because it was originally barked at us in Afrikaans, here goes, "You stupid asshole if you don't shape up I'll tie your dick around your neck and then chase a nude whore past you, until you choke yourself to death!" Another one " If you don't shape up shithead I'll jump down your throat, shit on your lungs, and then charge you for bad breathe, do you understand!" Funny now but not after you have been training for hours in the hot desert.

Another master of the English language (sarcasm) was our Afrikaans sergeant Potgieter who needed to explain what to do at funerals, "Ok chappies remember when a 'reverse' comes past, stand in a straight stripe in pairs of three 'comes' to 'detention' and salute the stuff inside."

Telling these stories later with friends would make us choke with laughter, and there were many more that I can't remember after all this time. This was the first time that I mixed openly with Afrikaners and was called 'Jood' or Jew by many of them in a friendly sort of way. The pet Jew! I have to say that I did not take any crap from them, and after a few fights, I gained respect.

Being quite a good athlete they left me alone most of the time. There was another Jewish guy with the last name Katz. He was picked on constantly but he knew how to act stupid. They would make fun of him and say in Afrikaans, "Jy is amper a mense Katz", you are almost a person Katz, meaning that when he finishes his army training he will become a person. Katz did pretty well because he could make them laugh.

Angry Enough to Kill

One day after training for hours in the hot desert we sat down for lunch in the field dining tent. I was very hungry and started to eat. I had also forgotten to remove my bush hat which was a no no when you ate. This officer saw me and came up to my table. Without saying anything he took my drink and poured it all over my food. If there was ever a moment that I wanted to kill somebody, that was it. I was not allowed to get more food so I just ate it. I got him back just before I left the base, you will read about it later.

Afrikaners Talking About
Blacks in the Army

Many times I would listen to Afrikaans guys talking about blacks. This one time I heard these guys discussing whether blacks were human or not, and if they deserved to be classified as humans. There was one Afrikaner with a conscience who kept saying but they are people too according to God. There was an element in the Afrikaner community that considered apartheid to be appalling, but were too afraid to speak out.

English Speakers Were Called 'Soutpiel'

In the army all the English speaking guys were referred to as soutie or soutpiel, meaning salty penis or salty dick. The explanation goes as follows; you speak English and live in South Africa .

One leg is in South Africa, and one leg is in England, and your penis is touching the salty ocean. Hence salty penis or soutpiel.

There was a rift between the Afrikaners and the English that they never forgot. About a 110 years ago the British put Afrikaner men, women, and children in concentration camps and many died. They never forgot it.

The Afrikaners considered themselves as the 'Boers' meaning farmer or pioneer of the country which the British tried to control, hence the rivalry!

*2ⁿᵈ from left during a break from
training in Upington 1975*

Training for War

We trained shooting our rifles, throwing grenades, and practiced stabbing the enemy with our bayonets. They would reinforce it with you have to kill that black guy, because if you don't he will kill you and your family. By doing this they dehumanized the enemy as being black and extremely dangerous. This would leave us with no doubt what you had to do if we encountered any black soldiers. All you could remember was that he will kill you and your family. We knew what we had to do. Running in the morning, marching until noon and training until dinner. After that it was night training. I hated it at first but later got used to it.

Every Friday night the Jewish guys were allowed to go out of the base for the Sabbath. All the Jewish families in the town couldn't do enough for us. I was special being born there, and everyone knew my family. We were fed the most amazing dinners and treated like royalty until 9 o'clock, the time we had to be back in the base.

Horse School

I was about to learn something new in the army, and that was never to trust anyone again. One day some officers arrived at our base and were looking for some good soldiers to go to horse school. Wow, I heard that horse school was great, nice dorms, great food, lots of passes to go home, and best of all I loved animals.

They gathered all the soldiers in my base together and told us they were looking for some good soldiers to go to horse school. At that moment our officer shouted, "Around the magazine." This was our signal to run around a fenced off area of about a quarter mile that secured all the ammunition and weapons on the base. My understanding was that the first few soldiers to run around the magazine, would be off to horse school. Out of about 150 soldiers I came in around 4th or 5th, and was sure I was off to horse school.

Well as it turned out they took the last 5 or 6 guys that came in. These guys couldn't run and were considered no good for the infantry, so off to horse school they went. I was so disappointed!

A funnier story that stopped me from volunteering for anything again goes like this; one day after lunch they asked us if there were any musicians among us. Again, I thought I play guitar, I'm pretty good, this could be a great way to get out of this base. I knew they needed musicians for army bands. I volunteered and they took all 6 or 7 of us to the other side of the base.

It took us over two hours to move an enormous piano from one side of the base to the other. When we got back to our tents, totally exhausted, all the other soldiers laughed and made fun of us.

My volunteering days were definitely behind me for good!

To the Border and War

Being tough, which you had to be, we continued training. Then one day out of the blue, we were told to pack all our stuff, and that we were going to the border that evening. No one knew what was going on but we packed and got on the train for the border area in north Namibia, which South Africa controlled. Traveling by train I witnessed one of the most disgusting things in my life. One soldier pulled out a huge sharp knife and said he was going to kill a black guy, cut off his testicles and make a little pouch for himself. I looked at him shocked and thought I had seen photos of things like this perpetrated by the Nazis. Everyone laughed and thought what he had said was funny.

I am not sure if they thought it was funny, or if it was that group mentality thing!

Cruelty on the Train

Something else my army buddies thought was funny, was to heat up coins and throw them to starving black children, begging on the railway tracks. As they caught the money it would burn their hands and they would scream and cry, which would cause all these guys to roar with laughter.

Yep, these were my soldier buddies whom I needed for protection in the future, and was not aware of yet!

When we arrived at our destination, many infantry bases from all over the country were already there. We were about three thousand men herded into a big hall and visited by PW Botha a South African politician soon to be the Prime Minister. The year was 1975 and he would become South Africa's leader three years later.

He told us that we were about to enter Angola unofficially, which was a few miles north from where we were. He also told us that it was volunteer, and whoever did not want to go could step forward. Everyone laughed nervously, but nobody dared stepped forward.

We had just found out that we were going to war, but who were we going to fight? We were a very well trained and a powerful army with many weapons and not afraid to use them. There was no media and if they were around they would have been escorted out politely!

Me on the border of Namibia about to enter Angola 1976
Can't remember why I was so thin

Farmer Killed by Terrorists

While waiting to go into Angola there was some trouble on the border and our unit was called to investigate. We got our equipment and were dispatched to a farmhouse. As we arrived at the farm we saw a woman and her four year old daughter holding each other and crying. Her husband had been shot by terrorists and he was slumped face down against a wall with bullet marks going up from his body to the top of the wall. His dog sat down next to the body and refused to leave his master's side. Everything looked so peaceful except for this violent scene that unfolded in front of us. It was a shock seeing this for the first time, but I would see more in Angola. Another South African unit followed these terrorists into the bush with a helicopter. We were informed later that they caught 3 terrorists, and that they were executed on the spot.

Going into Angola

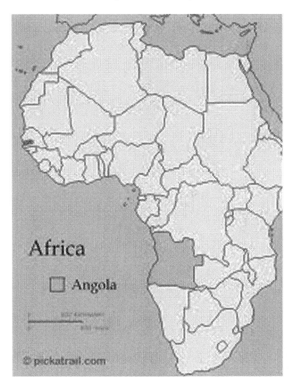

Angola in Africa

Two days later we loaded onto 'Unimogs' Mercedes trucks with a 24 gear range and traveled through the bush to a base camp on the border of Angola. Our mission was to support a South African Infantry base that was moving forward to confront the enemy in Angola. The enemy were civilian Cubans that were forced to fight for the Soviet Union. There were also different political groups that fought with us, one was UNITA . The other two forces that opposed us were, the FNLA, and MPLA assisted by the communists.

As we entered Angola all we could see was a barrage of weapons and ammunition lying around everywhere. The Portuguese some of mixed race did not get along with the blacks in Angola, "We hate the blacks" they would say as they passed us traveling south toward South Africa for sanctuary. They saw themselves as being better than the indigenous people. The feeling was mutual both ways.

The Unimogs that carried us into Angola

There were cars burned out with bullet holes all along the road. Suddenly we saw cars racing towards us! They were Portuguese refugees fleeing for their lives. They told us that they were lucky to have gotten out. They were allowed to leave and as a warning not to return, they said that black soldiers had broken their children's arms.

**Rob the medic and I taking a breather
in an Angolan village**

Dead Cubans

A few days later we drove past an open field with a horrific smell and were told that the South African army had slaughtered about 3000 Cubans in a fire fight two days before. We could smell their bodies rotting. We starting to realize that this was going to be an extremely difficult time.

One day we came upon a cheese factory. As we entered, we could see a cheesy substance all over the factory floor, and jackets still hanging on hooks in the offices. The workers had run for their lives when they found out that large groups of Angolan troops were heading their way.

We Blow Up a House

The South African army had no hesitation about using force on civilians. We were in a town and suspected that there were enemy soldiers holed up in a house about 200 yards up ahead of us. The army told everyone to come out with their hands up or they would destroy the house. Now we did not know if there were children or women in the house, and after about 10 minutes with no answer, we brought in a tank which basically leveled the house and everything in it, blowing pieces about a quarter mile into the air. We moved on around Angola from place to place, week after week. I didn't wash or shower for three months. They gave us half a helmet of water each day.

This was to wash our faces and then brush our teeth, and you had better do it in that order! We were allowed to grow beards and when the seams that held our clothes together rotted we were issued new fatigues. We slept in one man tents. The weather and terrain is very similar to that of Hawaii, beautiful and it poured every afternoon.

Beauty of the Angolan landscape

A Man With no Shoes

While we camped out near some village off the beaten track, relaxing with some friends I heard this groaning and looked up. I saw this black man of about 65 limping towards us, and he looked like he was in agony. He had no shoes on and had a difficult time walking. The area we were in had a great deal of sharp stones all over the ground. As he got closer I could see he was in a great deal of pain because the stones were cutting into his feet. He got close to us and sat down gesturing that his feet were hurting. I remembered that I had an extra pair of army boots with me. Our medic checked him while I got the boots and put them on his feet. They were about 3 sizes too big, but he was happy just to have shoes. He grabbed my arm in a gesture of thanks with tears in his eyes. I laced the boots onto his feet and helped him up. As he started to walked I could see a smile appear on his face, and then he started to scream with delight and took off waving and shouting. I know it must have been a relief for him. I must admit it felt great helping another human being relieve his pain, and at least I was helping somebody in this unforgiving environment.

A 'Prehistoric' Village in Angola

We would go on patrols into different parts of the bush in Angola. On this particular day we patrolled about fifteen miles into the bush from a main road. We eventually came upon this village. All the people were wearing loincloths and lived in grass huts. I noticed that a lot of the tools were made of stone. As we entered the village the chief met us and wanted us to have a meal with him. He also offered one of our officers one of his wives. The officer respectfully declined and when we got back to our field base everyone made fun of him and asked him why he didn't take up the offer. He just sneered and walked away. It was an eye opener for me seeing people still living in a stone age environment. It was a learning moment, I never forgot how different people are all over the world. Seeing this made me realize how lucky I was to live the life I live, and I still appreciate it. Seeing these things in life especially when you are young, stays with you forever!

Veggie Butcher

Me, being a vegetarian makes this story funny. Two guys in my platoon caught a wild chicken and decided that it was going to be lunch. We were issued with big pangas or machetes for the jungle. One of these guys laid the chicken down on the ground with the aim of cutting its head off. Well his aim was not great and he missed a couple of times with blood spurting everywhere the poor chicken going crazy trying to get away. I felt so bad for the chicken that I grabbed the panga and chopped the chicken's head clean off. They wanted to make me their official butcher for the future. I respectfully declined the offer!

Entering a Deserted Village in Angola

One day we arrived at a totally deserted village, very surreal! The only guy there was a Portuguese speaking farmer who told us that he refused to leave. We warned him that when the Soviet backed armies come into his village they would kill him and his children, rape and then kill his wife. This guy took a liking to our medic Rob and myself. He invited us for dinner one night. His house was very beautifully decorated on the inside. While we were eating dinner I suddenly realized I was sitting in this comfortable house in the middle of a war zone with deserted houses all around us. I think later we convinced him to leave. He wanted me to swap my FN rifle for his beautiful Spanish shotgun. I was prohibited from doing so, but someone managed to get him an army weapon from somewhere.

We Owe our Lives to our Captain

Our leader, a captain who was very astute. He knew when to get the hell out of an area he suspected to be insecure.

I can say we owe our lives to him. He would send scouts to the top of surrounding hills to see if there were soldiers on the other side. Sometimes they would spot our scouts and start shooting at us. Our job was to back one of our infantry units that was always ahead of us, and if for some reason they were somehow overpowered we would move into their position.

There was pretty much no chance of that, but we were still shot at and bombed occasionally. Every night when we stopped we were told to dig four feet deep trenches and sleep in them. On this one particular night we heard guns going off in the distance. Yes, they were shooting at us from a distance of about 15 miles. Thirty seconds later shells started falling everywhere, the closest one about 40 yards away. My body started to shake and my heart pounded with fear. You can never explain the feeling, it is something you can only experience personally. Every time they fired at us, our bodies would shake with fear hoping that we would not be blown to pieces.

The Rape

After about two months we had seen some horrific killings of civilians and dead soldiers in different parts of Angola. We kept moving north toward the capital, Luanda. One night we stopped near Lobito in Angola and we all camped out in this village. Some guys started to drink beer, and got quite drunk. The army provided beer to the soldiers, go figure!

One of the guys in my group said he saw a black guy in a white shirt watching us. We all grabbed our rifles and chased him along a path that led to a house. At that time we were not sure if he was in the house, but did not want to take any chances, so one guy kicked the door in. We searched the house and eventually entered a bedroom. There were two people in the bed. We ordered them out because we were afraid that there were weapons in the bed. Somebody pulled back the blankets and we saw a teenage boy and girl in the bed. There were no weapons and the girl was nude. They were both shaking with fear thinking that they would be killed. I remember we took the boy out and I tried to calm him down.

What happened next caused me to despise some of my 'buddies' even today. One guy decided he was going to rape the girl. Everyone was tense and nervous with rifles and grenades, and none of us stopped him. The girl cried while he raped her then he came out and we left the house.

For years afterwards I kept asking myself why I did not stop him. We were young and nervous, trained to kill, but I still can't understand why I did nothing.

This incident made me extremely bitter and I had difficult time speaking to this guy again. We kept moving forward toward Luanda the capital.

Brutality in Angola

Another brutal incident that I encountered was when this thin man walked toward our soldiers with his head covered with blood, and I mean caked on to his face and chest. He told us that he got into a conflict with somebody from another tribe or group. Apparently a machete was taken to his head and split open his scalp. The skin on his head was split open from his forehead to the back of his head, and you could see the bone. He was lucky that it hit him on skull and not on his neck, otherwise his head would have been severed. Our medic Rob gave him shots in the wound to dampen the pain, and then sewed up his scalp. After the treatment he was on his way as if nothing had happened. What a crazy place we were in!

Leaving Angola

Just exited Angola 1976. I am holding the dog.

South Africa was about to take the capital and we knew there was going to be a lot of killing. We were about 10 miles from the capital, Luanda, and then suddenly we got the order to pull back. After three months it looked as if we were leaving this beautiful jungle of weapons, booby traps, and dead bodies.

As fast as we moved in our unit was moved out. After a few days we were back in Upington. When I first arrived in Upington to begin my army service the base looked like a dry dust hole in the middle of the desert. Now it looked like a 5-Star hotel with beds, showers, and food from the mess. It was luxury, and we were all very grateful to be back. We all wondered whether we were going back into Angola again!

That weekend we got a four or five day pass, and they told us not to talk about Angola at home, which all of us did of course!

Smuggling a Rifle Out

A friend of mine decided that he was going to smuggle a rifle home that he had found in Angola. The night before our pass he jumped the fence of the base and buried it in pieces with 600 rounds of ammunition in plastic bags about 300 yards from the fence. It took him about three months to get it home because he would take it home a little at a time, piece by piece.

A few weeks after we were discharged, he wrote and told me that he had sold it to a farmer, because he was afraid of getting caught and going to prison.

The FN Belgium rifle -7.62mm bullet- that I used. An extremely powerful weapon that could make a hole in a railway track . Also the type that was smuggled out.

A Shiny Parker Pen

What was really great about the South African Army was that we all got a shiny silver Parker Pen for going into Angola! We were all excited about this fantastic presentation we all received for risking our lives!!! What a great gesture! What's even funnier is that I still have the pen after 35 years. Again funny stuff.

Going Home, Back to the Base, More Training

There was an airport right next to the base, and I boarded a plane for home, about a one and a half hour flight. It was beautiful being served cold drinks like a king, and the air conditioning on the plane was amazing. Wow, I was in heaven after being in Angola.

Nobody at home realized that we were in Angola, and some people told me that I was making up stories.

They eventually read about it in the newspapers.

I had a great time in Cape Town seeing all my friends, and then it was back to Upington to finish off my army service. Three more months to go!

As soon as we got back, the training started again and they took us to a place called Riemvasmaak, one of the hottest places on earth. Mirage jets would come in and bomb areas around us. They wanted us to see the damage jets could inflict on the enemy, it was devastating! We picked up pieces of shrapnel the size of a plate. This area is extremely hot, and lower than the Dead Sea in Israel. It was terrible, but being young and tough we got through it.

Yes, our officers were new and we did not respect them, as we were war veterans, and they were not. They still treated us pretty badly and we all resented them.

Going Home and Payback

Well the time went by and we were leaving for home the next day. Their last message to us was, "We'll see you again, you'll be back", most probably because of the war in Angola. The seed was sown right there, and I knew I was never coming back, basically I was done!

That night we packed our stuff but many of us were still very angry with the way we were treated. We knew we wouldn't see our officers again, because we had to be out of there by 4 a.m. that morning. Buses would take us to the railway station and we would be on our way home.

The new recruits would only be arriving by 1 p.m. that day.

Before we left we were going to pay our officers back for their bad manners and meanness. (Remember that drink that was poured onto my food during lunch because I didn't take my hat off!) We went into the commander's tent and broke everything we could find.

I am kind of embarrassed now but we urinated and defecated all over the tent.

By the time they got to the tent the next day we were well on our way home. Poor new Recruits!

Back Home

Being home was great, I was so happy being finished with the army. I swore that I would never complain about anything ever again in my life. That didn't last long as I slowly got back into civilian life. I didn't realize it at the time but I had acquired a dose of post traumatic stress disorder.

One night while with some friends, I drove my car down the main road in Sea Point at about 85 mph. The security police stopped me and were about to handcuff me and take me off to jail. I started to explain that I had just come out of Angola etc. Luckily one the police officers had been in one of the same bases, and asked me about it. After he was satisfied that I was telling the truth and that I must have seen some crazy stuff he released me.

I was relieved and had learned a lesson. Being home was great, but I had a difficult time adjusting to civilian life, and was wondering what I wanted to do with the rest of my life. I had no clue at the time.

I joined a company that fixed telephones and was going to be a telephone technician. I actually liked the work and training. They made us wear a white coat like a doctor at work which I liked, don't ask me why.

As the weeks went by I slowly started to adjust to civilian life, until I got home one day. There was a letter in the mail informing me that I had a 4 month camp coming up in about a month. I remembered what they had told us before we were discharged at the base in Upington, "You'll be back."

I did not want to go back, but what was I going to do. I knew there was no way out. At about the same time blacks started protesting against Apartheid, and also that they didn't want to learn Afrikaans in school. They saw it as the oppressors language. I could see the writing on the wall.

Suddenly it all made sense to me, I could not live in South Africa anymore. I did not want to raise my children in a country that I thought was going into a civil war. I had made my decision.

My Decision to Leave

I was young and knew nothing about the outside world.

What was it like to leave everything that was familiar to me, and live in another country? The thing that clinched it for me was going back into Angola to fight again. For what? For whom? I had no motivation to go to war again, and maybe get killed or maimed this time. I knew it was time to leave. I told my parents what I was about to do, and they supported me. Just where was I going to go. As things turned out, I had friends who had just come back from Israel.

They told me that they had been on a kibbutz in Israel, and had crazy wild drunken parties with women from all over the world. I knew instantly that was for me!

My mom had a cousin and she asked him to talk to me about what to expect in Israel. Well it was great, I went to his house and he told what I had to do. He told me to do this and that, and he said that if I listened to him I would be okay. I listened and asked questions for about two hours. It was great, all the information I needed until I found out the following day that he had never been to Israel.

Is that funny or what, but at the time I thought he was an idiot.

Still being paranoid after my army service I bought a revolver. Feeling vulnerable even in civilian life, I would go shooting whenever I had the opportunity. I sold it to a friend before I left.

Leaving Never to Return

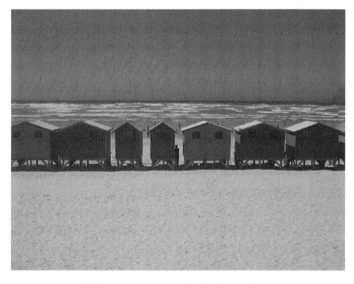

White as the sand of Muizenberg
Spun before the Gale

My parents bought me a one way ticket which was what I wanted. In my head at the time I did not want to return. I had just turned 21 and had no idea what was in store for my future. I only knew one thing was that I had to leave.

Well, January 16, 1977 arrived and I was packed and ready to leave. I had one suitcase and my guitar. That was it!

I said no goodbyes to anyone including most of my family. Maybe I was afraid that I would have broken down. My parents drove me to the Cape Town Airport and I boarded a jet for Israel via Johannesburg. I was sad to leave, but also very excited and looking for adventure. My Uncle Abe met me in Johannesburg before I boarded the airplane for Israel. I was very glad he came to see me off. The date was January 17, 1977. Walking to board the plane an official asked me why I did not buy a return ticket. I just looked at him and smiled, and instantly knew that he understood. He then waved me through onto the airplane. I must admit that at that moment I broke down and cried knowing that I was leaving everything that I ever knew, never to return.

Epilogue

Please contact me at pjhumme@hotmail.com if you have anything you would like to ask me or comment about in this book. I would be very happy to hear your thoughts about what I have written. I will answer any questions that you put forward to me about life in South Africa during Apartheid. I also wrote this book for my family, because these thoughts have been with me since I left South Africa, and I needed to put them on paper. I loved living in Cape Town, climbing Table Mountain, driving around the coast with my friends, going to beautiful beaches like Clifton and Muizenberg with their exquisite white sand and beautiful blue water.

South Africa is a beautiful land with a past of fire and blood. Hopefully it will come to terms with its tragic past.

About the Author

Philip was born and raised in South Africa. He grew up not having any social interaction with blacks as a child, or as a teenager because of Apartheid. He is also Jewish and experienced a great deal of anti-Semitism which affected him profoundly. After high school he was drafted into the armed forces and forced to fight in a war for the Apartheid Regime. Philip saw many terrible and tragic events that affected him deeply. He also goes through some of the most extraordinary events that engulfed him during his military service which eventually caused him to leave the country.

Made in the USA
Columbia, SC
11 September 2020